A Knack for Life

Poems by

Pamela Martin

A Knack for Life
Copyright 2009 by Pamela Gowan

All rights reserved under International and Pan-American copyright conventions. No part of this book may be reproduced, stored in a retrieval system or transmitted in any form, electronic, mechanical, or by any other means, without written permission of the author.

Illustrated by Kathleen Hardy.

International Standard Book Number: 978-0-578-01062-5

Table of Contents

Part I

Horatio 9
Ginger Vitus 9
Domestic Tranquility 9
The Cruciverbalist 10
Amoral Invalid 10
Destiny 10
The Bellicose Feline 11
On the Treadmill 12
Stay in School! 12
A Plutocracy? 12
Circus Circus 13
Only Time Will Tell 14
Unskilled Labor 14
The Reliquary 14
Miss Demeanor 15
A Basic Inequality 16
Penniless Pam 16
Ergophobia 16
My Bliss 17
The Demand 18
Villa Nova 18
Eureka! 18
In a Lurch 19
Senior Rita 20
Taciturnity 20
The Fantasy 20
"The Dead Poet Society" 21
Good Mourning! 21
A "Modern" Version of the *Turtle and the Hare* 21
Get a "Round Tuit!" 22
"B. Anonymous" 22
The *Glueteus Maximus* 22
The Cassandra 23
The Hopeless Romantic 23
"Know Thyself" 23
"Heart and Soul" 24

Part II

A Lonely Proposition 27
Delerium Tremens 27
That Proverbial Oxymoron 27
My Aromatherapy 28
Men 28
Too Much Interference...28
Cat Eyes 29
A Theory of Relativity 30
Pace Yourself 30
Take a Gander 30
Freedom Rocks! 31
Motion Sickness 32
Worrywarts 32
Arrested Development 32
The Nike of Samothrace 33
Poetic Advice 34
The Panacea 34
Diurnal Rhythms..34
"The Eight Hundred Pound Gorilla Never Sleeps" 35
Rhythm 101: Ah, Ha! or the "Ha Ha " Song...36
Rhythm 101: Oh, Ho! or the "Oh, Ho" Song..36
Rhythm 101: Da Da or the "Da Da" Song..36
Just Above Below Average 37
Frightful! 38
On dit 38
Superannuation 38
The Libertarian..39
"Pain and Suffering" 39
Uncommon Courtesy 39
Conspicuous Consumption 40
Sweet Nothings 40
Divine Retribution 40
A Forward Pass 41
Perjury! 41
"Leap Year" 41
Tendentious 42

Part III

The Busy Body 45
Said vs. Done 45
High Treason 45
"Going with the Flow" 46
Virginia, the Wolverine 46
Inner Dependence 46
"Grace under Pressure" 47
Sammy's Song (and Tabby, too!) 48
"In a Pig's Eye" 49
Predecease 50
The Tempest 50
I "Quote-a Quota" 50
Self-Employed 51
Inter-Course 52
Temporary Insanity 52
Elasticity 52
The Bright Knight 53
A Lethal Injection 54
Bob Barker 54
"Bad Fences Make Bad Enemies" 54
A Knack for Life 55
The Photogenic Past 56
Indecent Exposure 56
Decisiveness 56
The Architect of My Soul 57
"Non-Sense" as "Non-science" 57
Nihilism 57
Ostracism 58
"Sense and Sensibility" 58
Going to Extremes 58
In Denial 59
Transmogrification! 59
My Frisky Cats 59
Sublimation 60

Part I

Horatio

It's rude to be crude and lewd to be nude.
But you ought to know,
"There nothing either bad or good
But thinking makes it so."*

*Famous quotation from *Hamlet*, Shakespeare's *tour de force,* spoken by Hamlet's best friend and confidante, Horatio. Fain, I should have such a friend!

Ginger Vitus

My cat has halitosis.
It will strike you dead.
She doesn't brush her teeth
Before she goes to bed.
She has gingivitis
But is in denial.
She uses Listerine
Like it's going out of style.

Domestic Tranquility

I live with my ambivalence.
It is who I am.
I do my civic duty
For my Uncle Sam.
But I am quick to point out
The lack of clarity
When it comes to waging
War on poverty.

The Cruciverbalist*

"Nevaeh" is "heaven" backwards.
"Now" is a reversed "won."
"Evil" is to "live" recklessly.
"Wow" is a palindrome.
We do not play word games
As much as they used to
In the nineteenth century.
They had nothing else to do.

*A crossword puzzle enthusiast.

Amoral Invalid

"Who is to say
What is right and what is wrong?"
These are the final words
To my favorite song.
I sing it in the shower
And before I go to bed.
Every book is a good book.
That is what I said.

Destiny

We take many risks
As we go through life.
We start by getting up
And turning on the light.
You can't get more fateful
Than a fatalist.
But free will still awaits you.
I am sure of this.

The Bellicose Feline

Let's do the "paw jab"
Right in your face.
Then take one step back
And try to erase
What you have done
When mom comes home.
Cats are like people.
You can't leave them alone.

On the Treadmill

I have taught you everything
You may need to know.
Now that you are ready,
It is time to go.
When you embark on your journey
Remember what I said:
"Always tread lightly
Wherever you may tread."

Stay in School!

I memorized the words
To each and every song.
When I hear a ballad,
I adroitly sing along.
It really is amazing!
If I only knew
Math and science just as well,
It would be too cool.

A Plutocracy?

When I look around,
What is it I see?
Faith, hope and charity
Or abject poverty?
You would not believe me
If I said to you:
Life is for the living
Not the chosen few.

Circus Circus

Does it stay in Vegas
When you go home?
Or does it follow you
To the dead zone?
When things get complicated,
Let your conscience be your guide.
Vegas is everywhere.
There's no place to hide.

Only Time Will Tell

Give me life! Give me hope!
Give me everything!
Give me wealth untold!
Give me diamond rings!
But in the quietest moments
I will have my doubts.
Money can't buy happiness.
Just let me, please, find out.

Unskilled Labor

When I quit school, I was a fool.
Who couldn't figure it out?
I cannot read. I cannot write.
I am a dropout.
I can't find a job. Even the mob
Does not want to hire me.
It is too late to change my fate.
Now God wants to fire me.

The Reliquary

Take it from a professional,
You're an amateur.
Give it some time. You will do fine.
You can be a *saboteur*.
In our own way, it's safe to say
We are all but mercenaries
Toiling away until that someday
When we rest in Victorian cemeteries.

Miss Demeanor

When they were giving out "Looks," I thought they said, "Books,
I said, "Give me a creature feature."
That's what I got and I like it a lot.
Now I am a teacher.

A Basic Inequality

The time has come
For me to say
I must go
My separate way.
But separate but unequal
It will be
Because you own
The company.

Penniless Pam

It's true I have no money.
I'm penurious.
But mighty is the pen
That is curious.

Ergophobia

I often wander down the path
Of the conditional clause.
What if I had married
Mr. Santa Claus?
Would it make me happy
Working half a year?
Or would I still be sitting here
Crying in my beer?

My Bliss

Sammy likes to play the game of
Catch-me-if-you-can.
Tabby likes to play Tidily Winks
With a rubber band.
I like to sit and watch
In an armchair.
If there is more to life
I'm simply unaware.

The Demand

Tell me this.
Tell me true.
Did I mean
A thing to you?
Or was I just
A silly game?
Tell me now.
Please, explain.

Villa Nova

I live in a cottage
Overlooking the sea.
I can see it
But it can't see me.
That is the way
I like it to be.
The clandestine life
Is so good to me.

Eureka!

Take it from me.
I need it bad.
It is the best sex
I ever had.
Indulge me now.
I cannot wait.
I've finally found someone
To celebrate!

In a Lurch

When I hold my dear Sammy,
She's in repose.
When I hold my dear Tabby,
She squirms like a hose.
That's why I take my sweet Sammy
With me to church
And leave my poor Tabby
Swinging a birch.

Senior Rita

Sex is overrated.
It's a passing fad.
It's great when you're young
Even when you're mad.
But less and less often
You get around to it
Until soon you find
You can no longer do it.

Taciturnity

Religion, sex and politics
Are subjects taboo
To Pamela Martin
Although sometimes I do
Need a diversion
From the usual fare.
But I do not relish them.
I use them with care.

The Fantasy

I give to you kisses.
What you give to me
Is so overwhelming.
It's heavenly.
I try to ignore
How you make me feel
Because I know in my heart
That you are not real.

"The Dead Poet Society"

I take great umbrage
With those who say
I am all work
And no play.
"The play's the thing,*"
Prince Hamlet once said.
But what did he know?
He soon was dead.

*Hamlet: "I'll have grounds/More relative than this—the play's the thing/ Wherein I'll catch the conscience of the King."

Good Mourning!

It's six o'clock
And all is well.
You wish I'd just go
Straight to hell.
You were in REM*
So stolidly.
"Why don't you
Just leave me be!"

*A deep sleep characterized by "rapid eye movement."

A "Modern" Version of *The Turtle and the Hare*

I took a carriage.
You took a train.
But we both got there
About the same.
The train was robbed
By two masked robbers
Who got away with
The Jolly Roger's.

Get a "Round Tuit!"

I think it is a crime
That I write silly rhyme.
Anyone can do it
If he gets "a round tuit."

"B. Anonymous"

I have filled another page.
Have I proved myself a worthy sage?
If you think you do it better,
Send it in an unsigned letter.
The truth is but a school for scandal
And often is too much to handle.
The messenger is already dead
Before the book is completely read.

The *Gluteus Maximus**

Miss Demeanor! Miss Demeanor!
Would you call on me?
I would like to know
Where you get the energy
To get up in the morning
And stand before our class?
When you write upon the board,
We're looking at your ass.

*Latin, the largest gluteal muscle in the buttocks.

The Cassandra

"The best years have come and gone.
This, my friend, is it.
There's nothing more to say or do.
It is time to quit,"
Said the gloomy prophetess,
Who was so bereaved.
She had the gift of prophecy
But nobody believed.

The Hopeless Romantic

I have been a victim
Of an unfortunate circumstance.
I was born in a time
That killed all romance.
Romance is a novel
That you read in bed
That you would be better off
Never to have read.

"Know Thyself"

You don't have to tell me.
I have been a fool.
If I knew then what I know now
I would have stayed in school.
Illiteracy is bad.
Innumeracy is worse.
Ignorance of knowledge
Is a lifelong curse.

"Heart and Soul"

I don't have to tell you
I have done my best.
Even if I studied,
I couldn't pass your test.
I may be a dummy.
I may not be smart.
But I know for certain
I have a good heart.

Part II

A Lonely Proposition

I'm going straight to heaven.
You're going straight to hell.
I must admit
It suits me very well.
Once I get there
I will be on my own
Because I know
I will be all alone.

*Delirium Tremens**

Murray was her name
And I was to blame
When she became
Inebriated.
I did my very best
To give her rest
But she beat her chest
Infuriated.

*Latin, literally "trembling madness;" one of four categories of "alcohol withdrawal syndrome" characterized by hallucinations, confusion, autonomic hyperreactivity, and fever.

That Proverbial Oxymoron

I'm very serious
About my levity.
Comedy or drama,
What difference can there be?
Drama is something
That makes me shout.
But humor is something
I can't live without.

My Aromatherapy

I am writing faster
And more furiously.
This happens when
I don't have my tea.
Tea is very calming.
It puts me to sleep.
But I still have
Promises to keep.

Men

I take command
Of every situation.
I am brave
With insatiation.
Intrepid is the word
That best describes me.
But when I go home,
I'm a baby.

Too Much Interference

There is a code of silence
That separates us.
It is something
I always wanted to discuss.
But this silence
Speaks louder than words.
I have to say
It sounds absurd.

Cat Eyes

Tabby can play
"String" when it's dark
When there is not
One sparkling spark.
Night vision is something
Cats can't live without.
Otherwise they would
Thrash all about.

A Theory of Relativity

Rich is better
And poor is poor.
These are disparities
We can't ignore.
But when you try
To even the score,
The rich get richer
And the poor stay poor.

Pace Yourself

I do not have to tell you
You're a moron.
But do not listen to me.
I go on.
To digress is to travel
To another place.
I say it's better
If it changes the pace.

Take a Gander

A Secret is a secret
Until it is known.
Then it's a scandal
That is full-blown.
A scandal is better
If it is true
Unless, of course,
It happens to you.

Freedom Rocks!

Definite or infinite.
It's all the same to me.
Life is indeterminate.
So let me be.
I love you
And my country.
It feels so good
To be so free.

Motion Sickness

What goes up
Must come down.
And this world
Keeps spinning around.
When I get dizzy,
I am a fiend
If I don't have
My Dramamine.

Worrywarts

To prognosticate is to pontificate
As a doctor.
I stole the test
Right from the proctor.
Some of the time
We are too sorry.
But most of the time
We only worry.

Arrested Development

I was born
In the "Prairie State."
But to no one
I can relate.
There's something wrong
With my "indoor fins"*
Because I am
An orphan.

*i.e. endorphins, which are, and I quote, "any of a group of peptides that occur in the brain and bind to the same receptors as morphine, thereby inhibiting pain." (OED)

The Nike of Samothrace

        I live in a state of grace
       Enamored by the human race.
    I played the game and I have won.
       Now I'm having so much fun.
       To the victor belong the spoils.
   But do you know why my blood boils?
    Because, like Moses, I have no plan
    To enter into the "Promised Land.*"

*The "Winged Victory" of Samothrace (a Greek island) is the third century B.C. (c. 220-190 B.C.) marble sculpture of the Greek Goddess Nike (Victory). Since 1884, it has been prominently displayed in the Louvre where it has been one of the main attractions. But because Nike predates Christ, she technically can't enter the Christian section of heaven.

Poetic Advice

When the annotation
Is longer the poem,
It is time
To get going.

The Panacea

It's hard to say
If it will work.
All I know is
It will hurt.
But such suffering
We must endure,
If we are
To find the cure.

Diurnal Rhythms

I think I have proven
My not so subtle point.
Each day is a new day
When you're in the joint.
Is it old wine in new jars
Or new wine in old?
The answer you find
Will one day unfold.

"The Eight Hundred Pound Gorilla Never Sleeps"

Cicero and Caesar
Are now long gone.
But we remember them still.
They linger on
In the collective consciousness
Of our society.
They are living proof
Of immortality.

Rhythm 101

Ah, Ha! *or* The "Ha Ha" Song

Ha ha ha ha ha ha ha,
Ha ha ha ha ha.
Ha ha ha ha ha ha ha,
Ha ha ha ha ha.
Ha ha ha ha ha ha ha,
Ha ha ha ha ha,
Ha ha ha ha ha ha ha,
Ha ha ha ha ha.

Oh, Ho! *or* The "Ho Ho" Song

Ho Ho Ho Ho Ho Ho Ho,
Ho Ho Ho
Ho Ho Ho Ho Ho Ho Ho,
Ho Ho Ho.
Ho Ho Ho Ho Ho Ho Ho,
Ho Ho Ho.
Ho Ho Ho Ho Ho Ho Ho,
Ho, Ho, Ho.
"Merry Christmas!"

"Da Da" *or* The "Da Da" Song

Da da da da da da da,
Da da da da da.
Da da da da da da da,
Da da da.
Da da da da da da da,
Da da da da da.
Da da da da da da da,
Da da da.

Just Above Below Average

Vertically challenged
I will always be.
I'm about average,
About five-foot-three.
People look down
Their long noses at me.
I only wish
Someone would notice me.

Frightful!

I scare you.
You scare me.
We both scare
So easily.
You're afraid
I will stay.
I'm afraid
You'll go away.

*On dit**

I don't turn my computer off.
It goes in hibernation.
But it is ready when I write
The briefest salutation.
The energy I save
Is commensurate
With the time I waste
When I gossip.

*Latin, "a rumor or a bit of gossip."

Superannuation

When you have neuropathy,
You're not all that you can be.
When your motivation is low,
You may need a cup of Joe.
When you're tired and worn out,
You may need to jump and shout.
If you are not animated,
You will soon be carbon dated.

The Libertarian

I thrive on negligence.
Can't you see
How gosh darn happy
It has made me?
Ignore me if you will.
I do not care
Because I do believe
In *laissez faire*.

"Pain and Suffering"

I'm a glutton for punishment,
A sadomasochist.
And you are always
First on my list
Of those things
I have to do.
When I need pain,
I think of you.

Uncommon Courtesy

I would be discourteous
For me to say to you,
"I'm a giraffe
And you're a kangaroo."
I would not stick my neck out
So you could bounce around
In the "land down under."
It would make me frown.

Conspicuous Consumption

Do not consume
Such worldly things
As Irish coffee
And diamond rings.
Happiness comes
From deep within.
And that is where
You should begin.

Sweet Nothings

I was half.
Now I'm whole.
Now I have
One simple goal
That is to make
One last entreaty.
Darling, it's true,
You simply complete me.

Divine Retribution

There is nothing
I want more
Than to settle
Up the score.
But "revenge is mine," saith the Lord.
It is bittersweet.
That only makes me want it more
The faster my heart beats.

A Forward Pass

What would you do if I don't want to
Look the other way?
Would you protest me and then arrest me
But grant a final stay?
If I were you what I would do
Is to try not to molest me.
And in the end I say to you
You should not detest me.

Perjury!

You must admit that in a fit
I do what I can
To tell the truth although a sleuth
Would not understand.
There are times I do believe
Simple truths should go unspoken.
And that is why even I
Say the legal system is broken.

"Leap Year"

Whatever happened happened.
That's the way it was.
Misery loves company
I should know because
We are judged by the company
Daily we keep.
Even so you ought to know
Love is a leap.

Tendentious

A proclivity is a propensity
Of a negative kind.
Anyone who has one
Would be so inclined
To conceal his tendency
So unrefined.
It's as if we have to say
He's legally blind.

Part III

The Busy Body

What's more blatant than a latent
Feministic slur.
Don't look at me.
Look closely at her.
She is the one
Who won't wash your clothes
Because she's too busy
I suppose.

Said vs. Done

I am a true feminist.
But I am of that ilk
Who wears only stockings
Made of finest silk.
Nobody notices
That what I say and do
Are in perpetual conflict.
I know it is true.

High Treason

Never was there ever
A more chauvinistic slur
Than what he just said
Right in front of her.
I cannot repeat it.
That would denigrate
Everything I stand for
Just like Watergate.

"Going with the Flow"

I don't know the difference
Between what is right and wrong.
Honestly I say,
I just go along
With what the crowd says.
Surely they must know
More about current ethics.
How passively I go.

Virginia, the Wolverine

No one really knows me
The way I know myself.
That's the way I like it.
I am in poor health.
What I really want
Is just to be alone
And to finally have
A room of my own.

Inner Dependence

In reality,
I do not live alone.
I live with my father
In a loving home.
He didn't know what hit him
When I moved back in
But we know for certain
It was a win-win.

"Grace under Pressure"

I don't feel peer pressure.
I don't have a peer.
And that explains, in part,
Why it is I'm here.
Certainly rejection
Hovers all too near
When we venture forth
Into the land of fear.

Sammy's Song (and Tabby, too!)*

When she was a kitten
We were very smitten.
Hi-ho, the derry-o,
We were very smitten.
Now she has grown up
Like a Buttercup,
Hi-ho, the derry-o,
Like a Buttercup.
Now the cat stands alone
In our sweet home.
Hi-oh, the derry-o,
In our sweet home.
She plays along
As if nothing's wrong.
Hi-ho, the derry-o,
As if nothing's wrong.
She doesn't go to bed
Until she is fed.
Hi-ho, the derry-o,
Until she is fed.
The tail wags the cat
In an attack.
Hi-ho, the derry-o,
In an attack.
She is so cute.
There's no substitute.
Hi-ho, the derry-o,
There's no substitute.
She is the most.
I surely boast.
Hi-ho, the derry-o,
I surely boast.
I love my cat.
That is a fact.
Hi-ho, the derry-o,
That is a fact.

*As sung to the tune of the children's song or nursery rhyme,
The Farmer in the Dale (Dell).

"In a Pig's Eye"

The surest way to ruin
A perfectly good thing
Is to hear
Those old wedding bells ring.
This piggy went to market.
This piggy stayed home.
This piggy thought it better
To be alone.

Predecease

I do believe
In free competition
And that we should all
Shed our inhibitions.
That is to say
When I go to perdition
You will already be there
By your own admission.

The Tempest

You have given new meaning
To "tempestuousness."
I cannot believe
That your senselessness
Has led you to the place
That you now inhabit.
And I know for certain
It was a real gambit.

I "Quote-a Quota"

I "quote a" someone
When I have to explain
What I am doing
Out in the rain.
A "quota" tells me
When I have done quite enough
And when it's time to
To stop writing this stuff.

Self-Employed

I know what it's like
To work for someone.
I should know by now
With all the work I've done.
Some say it's better
But I say it ain't.
When you work for yourself,
You work for a saint.

Inter-course

You love her
And she loves you.
What are you
Supposed to do?
Marry her
And end it all
Or carry on
And have a ball?*

*The obvious answer is to do *both*.
Marry her *and* have a ball!

Temporary Insanity

I once was mistaken.
I made a mistake
When I gave to you
My heart to break.
This I know for certain,
I won't do it again.
From now on
You are my "friend."

Elasticity

A pig with lipstick is still a pig.
A fish out of water is still a fish.
A man without a woman is still a man
But he's more like a rubber band.

The Bright Knight

If only I could be as prolific
As Paul McCartney
And write a theme song
For a blockbuster movie.
I would consider myself
Such a success.
But, like Sir Paul,
I couldn't care less.

A Lethal Injection

Right attitudes and right actions
Equal achievement.
Wrong attitudes and wrong actions
Equal bereavement.
But mediocrity
Will always be
The essential quality
Of democracy.

Bob Barker

Love is for strangers
Who should know better.
If you ask me,
I need an Irish setter.
Man's best friend
Will always be
The one who's barking
Up his tree.

"Bad Fences Make Bad Enemies"

We simply cannot duplicate
The love we have lost.
We *can* pick up the pieces
But, God knows, the cost.
I told myself you could still
Be my closest friend
But I think that's impossible
Until the fences mend.

A Knack for Life

I have a knack for living
And a knack for life.
I have a knack for anything
That doesn't cause strife.
I have a knack for you
And a knack for me.
I have a knack for celebrating
History.*

*i.e. the "art" of history.

The Photogenic Past

Photograph your memories
With kodachrome
So when you are
All alone
They will constantly remind you
Of what was before
But, sadly enough,
Is nevermore.

Indecent Exposure

What could be more frivolous
Than going to the fair
And riding ponies all night long
In your underwear?
Don't you wonder why it was
People stopped to stare?
I can't see how you were
Completely unaware.

Decisiveness

The time has come
For those who know
Exactly where
They want to go
To get there quick.
But, even so,
They are walking
To and fro.

The Architect of My Soul

I couldn't care less
But maybe I could.
You know I did.
You know I would
Give you shelter
From the storm.
And I will keep you
Safe and warm.

"Non-sense" as "Non-science"

It remains a mystery
Why we study history
And learn those things time forgot.
But, then again, we know them not.

Nihilism

Enervation is the quality
That sets my spirit free.
It tells me I am nothing
And then it lets me be.
Lassitude is the one thing
I can't do without.
It tells me I am nothing
Beyond a shadow of a doubt.

Ostracism

A preponderance of the evidence
Only proves to me
You were somewhere
You weren't supposed to be.
Let's make it clear.
You must stay
Far from that place
Until Judgment Day.

"Sense and Sensibility"

We do what we can, if we can, when we can
But why
Do anything at all?
We only have to die.
But given the proper
Motivation
We can cause
A great sensation!

Going to Extremes

I am so fastidious
I won't even sit
Next to someone in a lounge.
I will have a fit.
Although it's hard to get real close
In proximity,
I can and do still love you
In extremity.

In Denial

Pardon me for saying
You are curmudgeonly.
And I do not say that
Begrudgingly
Because you do deserve it.
Even with your stealth,
You cannot deny it
Even to yourself.

Transmogrification!

I love to be loved!
I can't deny it.
See for yourself.
You really should try it.
It will change
Your whole attitude
After one
Brief interlude.

My Frisky Cats

I think I like them
Because they don't talk.
But I hear them anyway
When I walk the walk.
They will let me know
With the greatest subtlety
That it is time to eat
The greatest delicacy.

Sublimation

It is the bane of human existence
To do the wrong thing
And to cause
Great suffering.
But is there really
A right time?
If I only knew,
I would be sublime.

www.ingramcontent.com/pod-product-compliance
Lightning Source LLC
LaVergne TN
LVHW011430080426
835512LV00005B/366